Lean House

Lean House

poems

Marci Ameluxen

MoonPath Press

Poetry
ISBN 978-1-936657-09-4

Cover art: "House of Mettle"
digital photograph by Pd Lietz, Manitoba Canada
www.pdlietzphotography.com

Author photo by Lorraine Healy

Design by Tonya Namura
using Gentium Book Basic

MoonPath Press is dedicated to publishing the
best poets of the U.S. Northwest Pacific states

MoonPath Press
PO Box 1808
Kingston, WA 98346

MoonPathPress@yahoo.com

http://MoonPathPress.com

To Annie Nelson
1925–1996

Acknowledgments

Grateful acknowledgment is made to the editors of the following publications, in which these poems first appeared.

Becoming: What Makes a Woman (anthology, University of Nebraska-Lincoln Gender Programs)—"Urn"

The Dirty Napkin—"Mythology"

Floating Bridge Review #5—"On Filing an Antiharrassment Order Against Her"

Hospital Drive—"Urn"

Off Channel (Finalist, Midwest Writer's Mississippi Valley Poetry Contest)—"I Dreamed I Was the Egg" "Rain, Northwest Meaning" "Last Visit With My Mother"

The Mom Egg—"Visiting Frida Kahlo" (published as "My Mother Visits Frida Kahlo")

Passager (Honorable Mention Passager Poetry Contest)—"Men in White, 1967"

Waccamaw—"Her Purse"

Many thanks to all the people who encouraged me, read and commented on these poems and the manuscript numerous times in various renditions: Lois Parker Edstrom, Teresa Wiley, Suzannah Dalzell, Diana Deering, Judy Bierman, Ginny Sickles, Angela Ramseyer, Ann Gerike, Susan Rogers Berg, Callie Harvey, my wonderful mentor Lorraine Healy, and my sons Evan and Brendan who insisted on a group hug every time my manuscript was rejected. And to Ed, there at the beginning.

Table of Contents

Lean House

Part I

I have been thinking much about
you all summer and how we have
gone through the same troubles,
visiting the bottom of the world.
I have wanted to stretch out a
hand, and tell you that I have
been there, too, and how it all
lightens and life swims back...

Letter from Robert Lowell to
John Berryman, 1959

Offering

They are walking in snow

the mother pulls her small daughter

inside her coat

together their feet

   make the tracks of one animal.

Childhood Lexicon

Unbidden they live
in her drawings,
        minotaurs, ogres, cyclops,
her favored serpents,

some who dive and spout innocent water.

At the sitter's she grazes
through a giant Webster's,
        copies beasts and their unpleasant details:

        scales mounded on thorny bodies,
sharp claws (three toes in front

two in back), dragons with her mother's
green eyes.

In second grade her aunts, her teacher
        remark on her skill with a pencil,

        it whittles a figure to gray shades,
its point cool and sharp.

Mythology

the child was tiny   all things
were warm
including the river

then winter came   the river became ice
        the ice was imperfect and left a hole

there's nothing to do   the child's
doctor said, the hole's in her heart

it will murmur at the night

soon ice covered
all her world
another mother
        not her own
gave her a sweater
                of uncountable threads

each day the sweater
must be knit anew
        each night Penelope, unraveling,
shows her how.

Fairy Tale

There once was a small house
in a forest. It was brown.

Each day the curtains were pulled back
and the mother appeared in the window.

She held a spoon of clear broth
no
she held an arrow
no
she held an empty spoon
yes.

Soon the curtains were shut,
no light shown behind them.

But once a year when the mother
appeared at the window

its panes were washed and clear.
The mother smiled.

She held a spoon of rich stew.
The child ate knowing

tomorrow's spoon
would taste of dust.

Photograph of Them

He ties hemp rope on a sailboat deck,
       she stares from behind cat-eye sunglasses.
I am yet to bloom inside her.

They sit apart on the boat they have built together,
       they do not show if they are happy or sad.

No one can warn them
             these beloved.

Persephone Speaks

When will we be in our own home, mother,
this gray to lighten,
the sun to lean through our window
as we eat breakfast together?

We're caught in this dark world of gone:
        your beautiful mind
            my green years.

Braid my hair again, mother,
brush out the night I
feel growing inside me,

dirt is in my mouth
and beneath my fingernails.
Wash me,

scrub the skin and heart,
polish my bones
and I will be new again.

Caress me, your touch
is warm sunlight.

Speak, mother.
But your tongue is bound with the knots
of all you haven't said.

Childhood with Schizophrenic Mother

Each day a car wreck,
with my tiny strength I breathe
life, my mouth to hers.

Hospital: Interview With the Mother

In the small white room
they keep asking *"can you state
a current event?"*

My childhood was happy.

I remember fields of grain bending and growing.
I was afraid of spring, those deep
unplanted furrows.

I wanted to be a storm.
Snow in winter was a storm,
lake ice cruelly
chopped into blocks
to lie in summer sawdust.

Summer was heat and watermelon juice,
grasshoppers to fit your hand.

One day

the wheat stalks were broken,
every other one. After school
I skipped rope but my shadow
did not move with me.

There was noise and beauty.
Grasshoppers came, they spoke
and told me to rest, I was so very,
very tired, rest they said,
I lay in grass
and darkness lay beside me.

The Daughter Speaks

I know a few things   that *mother*
is a crushed flower

how desire breathes hollow as a bowl
does not conjure love

that the heart is an animal
            curled in a cave

I know some things   ruin
is a road

            a mother can
be a road

in the winter picture
            cold is cold

a little girl stands   shoeless
            my nameless mourner.

Iron

Grandma says
she says put the
butter on like this
sizzle goes the waffle
iron. Pour the batter
she says, I lift
the green jug
watch white batter like
thick cream hit
metal peaks, fill
valleys, spill over.
Close the lid, she says
steam rises   hiss
bubbles peek, dressed in batter,

wait, says grandma
then her blue-veined hand
with my small freckled one
join at the handle, lift together.
Take the fork like this
she says, we pierce
crisp waffle skin,

grant my plate its patient reward.
How gray your eyes are, grandma
I say, then
her forearm roped with muscle
lifts her soft hand to
smooth my hair

Yes, she says
they are gray like metal and
inside I am strong
and inside you are strong
like iron.

Mother Alone

i.
The dining table stands
by itself in the room, the walls

are yellow childhood.
One person sits there, smoking. I shout

for the curtains to open,
make darkness escape,

air hissing from a balloon.

ii.
My mother is ash falling
from her cigarette, a gray leaf

that knows no way but down.
I want to believe obedience

will make the story right,
monsters and witches slain,

ash unburned.

iii.
The trees outside take the shape
of her face and I'll know

next time to craft sweet words
with my tongue,

tuck the blanket under
her chin against the chill.

Men in White, 1967

Speak of the ambulance
that bears men in white
to the doorstep of a lean house:
there lives a mother

her mind a broken shell.
She strokes her face
as if it could help.
       Her eyes are shut to the walls.

There lives a small daughter.
She has already lived long
enough for her bones to feel
       what is not replaceable.

The men in white have crisp jackets,
their pants are creased.
They look big next to the mother,
well-fed,

yet they know to soft-touch
her elbow, gentle her
       like a calf at roping
       the whites of her eyes showing.

A needle floats
in the orderly's hands,
he points to the ambulance
       step inside please

and she is gone.

After—he is waiting and watching—
a man in a brown suit
fumbling
I'm your dad.

The Universe Sends a Message

I don't know how to put it into a poem,
her Steno notepads filled with the letters "DMV"
in large block print, the pressure hard
on the pencil,

        her happy interpretation "Drink More Vodka"
written in a dozen more notebooks,

what words to use for her empty apartment,
security deposit unclaimed
because there's no time to clean out a refrigerator
full of lemon meringue pies
and Coors Light,

our truck too small to haul away the damp mattress,
blue couch, blemished coffee table,
our escape home on an Oregon freeway, how to describe

the lightness, the release of laughter that is weeping,
when my husband and I see the sign at the same time,
"DMV - Department of Motor Vehicles"

a message un-cosmic, liberating,
the universe safe and mundane,
easy to understand after all.

Her Studio

After "Nantucket" by William Carlos Williams

Paintings through the doorway
eerie red and black faces

seen through a child's eyes—
Smell of turpentine—

Fogged light of a winter day—
On the wood stool

a gray palette, the paintbrush
hardened, by which

an ashtray is lying—And the
luminous, silent eyes.

Emptiness

It's not depression
I just have
>   *human*

some down days.
>   *silence*

Into my mind I carve
a space
>   *havoc*

hide what could become enormous
>   *swallow*

if I don't watch it.
I have a fine wool sweater
>   *ice*

to cloak my entrance.
No one knows the something
>   *mask*

not there. I can dress it
plain and simple.

Many times it's become
word   breath   line
>   *voice*

other times a beast
padding its paws against
my breast
>   *possession*

you'd be amazed how much I seem
to need it
      containment

construct bars on windows
filled with light.

Part II

While from the bottom of a pool
Fixed stars govern a life
                    Sylvia Plath
                        Words

Leaving

Each year she walked further away
mist gathered at her feet

then scrawled its gray name
on her thighs and belly.

Soon mist shrouded head   ears
eyes

all that was visible
was her open mouth.

The Berry Fields, 1974

In August these men come
        from the city to pick currants,
faced middle age but still young
        below the skin.

They shout greetings as I join them
        on the crumbling bus, a girl of fourteen
who braves the smell of malt liquor

to earn money for school clothes.
Those who still own tenderness
        offer it; the smiles,

the jokes, gentle pushes to my shoulder
as to a little sister.

In the fields I lean over rows beside them:
the vet, dark prisoner of his scroll tattoos,
chest bare under a leather vest,

Indians with broad planed cheeks, flushed,
stiff hair pulled back with a cord

or with a bandana on forehead, like Geronimo;
a small Phillipino man, his hat "U.S.S. Kitty Hawk"
        crushed to his skull, works silently and alone.

Currant juice prickles our arms, pant knees are worn
        from our supplicant kneeling;
we are all beggars here
but dignity knits us together,

this small family,
        impermanent, flawed.
It made me happy to be claimed.

On Filing an Antiharrassment Order Against Her

I stand at the government counter
to pay my eighty dollars,
complete the forms

that may stop her disturbed
visits to my workplace,
cease the midnight phone calls,

the puzzled inquiries from police
when she reports me kidnapped
by my husband.

This Order will place a wall
between our faces and divide our voices
but I would say to her now:

this is not the final page
of our book,
does not erase

your caresses that soothed nightmares,
does not wash away the Saturday
you sewed beads on my Camp Fire girl vest,

does not fade the day I waded
into the ocean and turned to see
you smile at me, red lipstick bright

against brown freckles.

Visiting Frida Kahlo

I *know* you met her.

The titles of your paintings reveal it,
journal your honeymoon trip—*Oaxaca,*
Cuernavaca, Tlaquepaque,
Mexico City, 1952, where Frida, unsteady,
greets you at her blue door,

her brows dark birds.
You hug as sisters, two who enjoy
a dirty joke, burn of good whiskey,
whose fingers twitch for cigarettes
and smooth wood paintbrushes.

Frida compliments your accent,
is pleased you can also chat in German
while monkeys watch from canvas leaves.
Diego brings wine in an earthen jug,
a bite to eat? he teases, then Frida

dismisses him—she values time with women.
From a bureau covered with sugar skulls,
feathers, bones, Frida brings out
her silver hairbrush: you unclip dark
strands gathered at the nape

of your slender neck.
With lean strokes she brushes your hair
murmuring folk songs, love poems,
brushing   brushing
as if you were a canvas,
rough yet full
of the skin of life.

I Dreamed I Was the Egg

Her hand is on her belly
        I am the pressure
against her palm

my body is lace
        braided in her womb

                new lungs breathing
        her cigarettes, smoke

hollowing me like a gourd.

Was there an ache in my planting
        that she became such
a reckless farmer?

Like a barnacle's
        feathery hand,
                my small fingers stroke her
with a beggar's touch.

I am rescue

                carved in a newborn's form,
still wet with the dew
        of her coupling.

Uncle Emil

When my uncle comes back from the dead
he is tired

his bed is still unmade   his sisters cry
in the corner.

He wants to know
          what happened to all the men
he tried to save

the South Pacific soldiers whose bodies
he reached into

their bone and tissue
dressing his fingers   his hands garbed

with their sinew.

He remembers binding them over and over

          and again over

brushing mud and insects away
          from the young blossom of their faces.

This day I cannot name
          what he could not rescue.

I ask him instead to remember
the marsh birds
          the kind who murmur and coo
in the evenings

could he listen to their trills
                    and forget

about the day he lay down
      his beautiful mind for them

for them all.

Love Poem With Bird

From our bedroom window you watch
all summer the mother
on her lichen-padded nest,
frail hummingbird swaying
on thin branches.

Like an Irish grandmother
you fret over the two eggs
tiny as pearls,
voice exuberant when
new beaks probe from
under the mother's wings.

Daily you urge the chicks' progress:
open swallow of mouths,
the first down turned to feathers.
They were your brave toddlers,

whirring wings as if crazed, standing
on nest edge, wobbly, tipping,
mere moments from falling.
One fledgling leaves, and that night

the wind blows hard, the lone chick
tumbles and clings to trunk bark.
You stand watch at our dark window
listening to wind, grieving,
worried for everyone's children.

Prayer

At night my hands stroke

              my husband's face

like the rosary   they trouble round bones

        of the skull   knobs of temple and forehead

                  hailed in procession

a crescendo   glides the husk of ear

       as jaw breeds mouth

                    it nourishes,

knuckles brush soft cheek with

               their forested angles

I have seen these eyes be wells of lament

        now soft lids shelter their orbs

and I recite each lash by memory.

Two Sons

1.
Blue eyes, towhead,
tumbling toddler in a grocery cart,
women came up to me at the store and said
"When he gets big the girls
are goin' *after* him."

Now eyes of milky longing
follow you through the sixth grade cafeteria;
you are still innocent.
Crossing from childhood

your face grows angular.
Neither of us have been
here before.

2.
Curly hair and root beer brown eyes,
    aged for eight years,
zooming on your bike
you ran over the cat
and thought you would go to hell.

An hour of wailing and tears
made your kitty okay.
Your mind of wonder asked:
How are tears made?
Do animals cry?
Do you hear with your mouth
    when it's open?

At dawn you are outside
cradling the cat like an infant,
whispering your own
Hail Marys, Our Fathers,
sealing your own ritual of forgiveness.

My Children Enact Complacency in the 21st Century

My son complains again
        about his turn with the dirty dishes

I think of the young girl who loved flowers
        my freckled grandmother

age eight and leaving her home
        to be a servant in a rich man's house

even as death smoothed the covers
        of her mother's bed.

Turtle

She lies at the bottom of the tank,
green and still, resting on colored
gravel. Her liquid eyes are

open. She does not move.
My son cries, asks questions with
no answers, then is quiet.

With his father's help he
finds a shoebox and prepares it
for her oval shell with a

trembling hand. A soft rag is chosen
from the bin. She is carefully
wrapped, corners tucked in just so.

His brother helps carry the box
to the woods, each holding a brown edge.
Between hemlock and alder they carve

a hollow with their shovels, place the
box and cast dirt with small hands. Soon
it is covered, and gray stones are mounded

like a quilt. After, my son names
her in a prayer, now companion
to others he once knew.

My 49th Year

The tape rewinds and I again,
her again,
big bottle, short—
no matter, clear or amber,

the clock ticks faintly
    I am safe?
Or her howls become mine,

voices to come from
                wall outlets
will they?

Doesn't a mother want a daughter
in her image.

Inter my sin—
I would not be her.

Rain, Northwest Meaning

I knew the forest duff like my own
smell, its dripping moss my sodden retreat.
I lay beside logs coy and warm, the sky
burned long branches to my eyes

and under me the beetles turning.
I knew that goat hooves are clipped or they
turn to rot, each hoof grown long would grab

the damp and wistful brown eyes beg mercy.
I knew the fisher girl who dropped a line into water,
her hook for bullheads, perch and the cat-eyed

dogfish, gray bellies slit pink by fisherman, their guts
ebbing.
When the white ferry bucked waves
to bring us to the city
I knew its wet streets and their colorless

panhandlers, fingers pickled with grime
and my mother embraced their need,
dropped crumpled dollars in their cans.

I knew my mother's morning dark,
brave bus rides to a dreary labor,
her evening escape sweet memory
frosted to the bottle
and coiled ruin in the smoke of her cigarettes.

Last Visit With My Mother

Strange weather that drenching rain in August
two weeks of sunlight only in steamy bursts

between showers. Fooled, the apple trees break
pink buds against season, gold stamens reach

for summer's waning light. Thrilled
bees clamber for blossoms around flushed

cheeks of ripe fruit.
A breeze troubles the leaves

and a single petal floats down to rest
against a fallen, still apple.

Her Purse

After she died
I looked through three mildewed trunks,
her possessions, the simple things:

a baby's rattle, brittle photographs,
a blue purse with lipsticks,
a compact

and a small plastic box.
Full of her teeth.
How long their roots!

I asked my husband to take
them to the landfill at night,
afraid someone would think

a whole life had been buried,
afraid the teeth
would form a mouth
and speak.

Um

They said *urn*
at the mortuary but it was a can,
shocking when laid in my hands
her years of life
dust to sift in a metal tube.

Like a kaleidoscope
I hold the can to my eye, see
spring flowers, a paint brush (turn)
bread, bottle of whiskey, music
(turn) scraped elbows, kisses.

How can we imagine the body
enkindled, cracked to immeasurable pieces,
soul left to remake
itself to colors,

bones of the hand white
July 4th sparklers,
red engine behind the hand
pulsing, then still.

Where to locate her last song,
cup between palms its breath
and note,

where to press and leave my print
on her tan flesh.

Visitations

We are camping by the beach
—myself, a husband, two sons—
and after the popping fire
lulls us to sleep

I waken to you unpacking groceries
by my sleeping bag.
I see you standing

in our old kitchen, its cheap
linoleum curling at the edges.
You smile,
eager to cook with me.

I smell you, your skin so close
I feel its warmth.

I remember your cigarette's smoke,
how its dark fingers circled your head,
sketched half-moons
beneath your green eyes.

But at night when you visit
your pink skin breathes whole.

You loved the ocean.
You do not speak.

Your silence is beautiful.

About the Author

Marci Ameluxen was born, raised and still lives in Washington State and for most of her life has lived on islands. When not taming her garden or writing poetry she works as a pediatric Occupational Therapist, and currently lives on Whidbey Island in Puget Sound with her husband and two children. Her poems have appeared in *The Comstock Review*, *Waccamaw*, *The Madison Review*, *The Compass Rose*, *The Dirty Napkin*, *Hospital Drive*, and *Crab Creek Review*, among others.

www.ingramcontent.com/pod-product-compliance
Lightning Source LLC
Chambersburg PA
CBHW022342040426
42449CB00006B/683